Rainbows And Rain: Finding Comfort In Times Of Loss

To order additional copies, please contact us.
BookSurge, LLC
www.booksurge.com
1-866-308-6235
orders@booksurge.com

PEGGY
WATERFALL

RAINBOWS AND RAIN:

FINDING COMFORT IN TIMES OF LOSS

2005

Rainbows And Rain: Finding Comfort In Times Of Loss

TABLE OF CONTENTS

For My Children,
Melody & Zachary

INTRODUCTION

I remember sitting at my desk in my home office, a few weeks after my father died, and realizing (in some kind of detached way) that it simply hurt to be. It wasn't what I expected. I'm not sure what I expected, but at the age of forty-two I think I believed that I should have been prepared to lose my parents. At one point or another, I'd lost aunts and uncles, grandparents, and even friends. I thought of myself as a reasonably realistic person, and the fact that my mother and father, in their late seventies, would not be around forever, was something I thought I understood.

I have never been so wrong.

I'm sure part of the reason it came as such a shock is because my father had just gotten re-married three weeks before he died. My brother and sister and I attended the beautiful outdoor ceremony on a sprawling piece of farmland in eastern Oklahoma. My father never seemed as alive and happy as he did that day. He was in extraordinarily good health, for a man of any age, and as I watched him and his new wife exchange their vows, it never occurred to me that it would be the last time I would ever see him.

When I got "the call" (everyone who gets "the call" seems to remember it with the clarity of fine crystal), I couldn't process what I'd just been told. "Please come home, Peggy. Your father is in the hospital and we think he's had a stroke. Please hurry." I lived in Atlanta at the time, and dropping everything and catching a plane to Oklahoma was about the last thing I expected to be doing that day. I told my daughter, Melody, then sixteen, to get on the phone and *find Jack*. Everything was happening too fast. I couldn't function. I couldn't even remember how to make an airline reservation. I needed Jack to be there; I just sat down on my bed next to the phone and stared unseeingly into space. My mind wasn't whirling, it had completely shut down.

When Melody got Jack (my lover and best friend and my rock) on the phone, I heard myself saying the words: "Dad is in the hospital. I need you here, now." To his credit, he didn't ask me any of the dozen questions that he must have been thinking. He merely said, "I'll be right over."

The next several hours were a blur, but I remembered I had to get it together long enough to go downstairs and tell my mother, who had come to Atlanta to live with me and my two children just three months before this happened. She and my father had what I always referred to as a "dysfunctional divorce." In other words, they remained in frequent contact, relied on each other, and cared deeply about each other for the entire twenty-five years since the split. When my father announced he was getting married again, my mother literally went nuts, followed by a bout of deeply debilitating depression (and I later realized, grief), that was worse than anything I had ever seen her experience. My mother, bless her heart, was not a particularly stable influence in my life, having suffered from various forms of mental illness as long as I can remember. I couldn't imagine what she was going to do after hearing that Dad was in a coma.

I told her as gently as I knew how, asked Jack to stay with her and the kids, and headed for the airport. Looking back, I can see now that I had no business behind the wheel of a car, but somehow I made it to the hospital in Stillwater, Oklahoma. My sister, Polly, who lived in Wichita, Kansas, had been there for several hours, as had Linda, my step-mother of three weeks. They both looked like hell. Linda's entire (and considerable) family was there in the ICU, along with several other friends and relatives.

Dad had apparently been at his storage unit clearing it out in preparation for moving in with his new wife when he succumbed to the 105° temperature and collapsed with heatstroke. Linda had gone looking for him when he didn't come home for lunch, and found him there, unconscious. I can't imagine how devastating that must have been for her. The paramedics had revived him three times with the cardiac defibrillator. He was in a comatose state, hooked up to more machines and tubes than I could have imagined possible. Seeing him like that broke my heart; I stayed glued to his side all night. Sleep seemed irrelevant, as my mind was completely occupied with the enormity of what was happening.

He never regained consciousness. Eighteen hours after I arrived, he was pronounced "brain dead" by the neurosurgeon on staff, a particularly jarring thing to be told about a man with a Ph.D. in electrical engineering from MIT. Everyone agreed that we had no choice but to discontinue the life-sustaining IV and respirator. We stood around his hospital bed and watched, as the most brilliant man most of us had ever known ceased to breathe. His heartbeat slowed, the numbers edging downwards on the monitor until slowly, agonizingly slowly, his heart came to a stop.

The funeral was packed with my father's colleagues, friends, and family, and my brother flew in from Australia. He and I each took a few minutes to eulogize Dad, and I still don't know how I got up in front of all those people and said all those eloquent things in a calm and strong voice. My sister, the journalist, wrote his obituary, as well as a moving and beautiful tribute piece which appeared that morning in the campus newspaper where he had been a professor for 35 years.

I was the executor for my Dad's estate, and it was amazing to me how much work it turned out to be. The phone calls, the letters of notification, the financial records, all of it seemed so unimportant, so irrelevant, and yet it had to be done.

It was after I had cleaned out my Dad's apartment, after most of the initial estate work had been done, after the flowers and cards stopped coming, when I realized that I had only just begun to grieve. That's when I realized, it didn't just hurt to talk about it, it didn't just hurt to miss him and not be able to see him, and it didn't just hurt to think about what it all meant: it simply hurt to *be*.

That was when I first realized that grief is about a whole host of feelings that are so much more complicated than mere sadness. Losing someone you love starts a ripple effect that extends to every part of our lives.

If that were my whole story, I doubt that I would be writing a book about grief and loss. As it turned out, losing Dad was just the beginning. Jack, the man I loved and shared my life with for nearly two decades, was diagnosed with terminal colon cancer a few months after Dad's death. He died less than a year later. My mother was unexpectedly diagnosed with bladder cancer exactly one week after Jack died, and passed away in hospice care just three months after finding out she was sick. This series of death blows rocked me to the core and I was determined to find some meaning in the confusion of it all. The decision to write this book came out of my own intense longing for answers and peace in the face of unspeakable sadness and bewildering emotional turmoil.

If you have experienced significant loss, you know that one of the most difficult things to deal with is finding words to go with your feelings. These "Grief Analogies" are intended to help you bridge that gap. No one knows your specific pain. I wouldn't presume to think that my experience mirrors yours, or even approaches the depths to which your sorrow extends. But it is my hope that somewhere in these chapters you will find a connection to the universally human experience of loss, and in-so-doing, realize that you are far from alone.

Author's Note: Most of the people presented here are real, but the names have been changed. In a few cases, the stories are compilations of the experiences of more than one person. Some of the stories are fictional in order to illustrate a point.

CHAPTER 1
Permission to Grieve Freely

What is it about our society that forces us to diminish our feelings of grief? Oh sure, it's acceptable for a while, but seriously, don't we all buy into the notion that we should get on with life after a while? We carry around a whole host of assumptions about how we should handle grief. I mean, after all, people die all the time, so what's the big deal?

Well, if you are reading this book because you are reeling from the death of someone you love, then you already know what the big deal is.

We don't handle grief, it handles us

If you've been to a grief support group, or read any number of books on this subject, you are doubtlessly familiar with the concept that grief is a process, not an event. Most of us are aware of the various "stages" of grief—denial, sadness, bargaining, anger, and acceptance. It's true, everyone I know who has gone through this has experienced each of those stages at one time or another. But if you are like me, that list of stages doesn't even begin to cover the wide-ranging reactions and responses that deep loss entails. I lost my father to a sudden death by heatstroke, my life partner, Jack, to a lengthy bout with colon cancer, and my mother to an alarmingly fast-moving bladder cancer. Each experience was completely different, which really surprised me. In the two years that followed, I have come to realize that every loss has its own unique qualities and that the depth of our grief is not predictable in the way we might suspect.

Different types of loss produce differing levels of grief

I think where we first get ourselves into trouble in this process is by making assumptions about how much grief SHOULD affect us. For instance, if you know someone who loses a parent, you might immediately assume that it must be very hard on them. But suppose they have been estranged from that parent for thirty years? Suppose the parent was abusive to them as a child? Or perhaps they were adopted? How does this color our expectations of the depth of a person's grief? The fact is, if we think we know we are very likely to be mistaken.

In my case, I was not what I would call "close" to my Dad, but I loved him. We had not had any major falling out or problems to speak of. The fact is, he was a difficult man to feel close to, so I rarely talked to him about anything of substance. We lived hundreds of miles apart and my life with my IBM career and my two teenagers was full without him. Frankly, I was completely taken aback by how deeply I was affected by his death. The main reaction I had was one of losing my footing, of suddenly not knowing what could be counted on in this life. The analogy: "The picture falling off the wall" is an attempt to express this startling reality that often seems to accompany the loss of a parent. Something that had *always* been there was no longer there, so I started to wonder what else I was taking for granted that might disappear tomorrow.

My sister, on the other end of the spectrum, was very close to my father. She lived nearer, for one thing, and saw him much more often. A recently divorced single parent, she relied on him for emotional support and help and advice on just about everything. When she lost him, it was absolutely devastating for her. This is what first got me thinking about how important it is not to assume that loss will affect any two people in the same way.

So, when a person loses a brother, sister, their own child, a spouse, or partner, everyone around them assumes that it is bound to be a cataclysmic event for the survivor. What about when our favorite aunt dies, or a neighbor who lives next door, perhaps a colleague at work? Our society tends to give us just enough space to grieve for a couple of days, tops. We might even have an enlightened boss who lets (lets!) us miss work to attend the funeral for a departed one from outside of our immediate family. But after the funeral, certainly within a few days or weeks, we are expected to be completely back to normal and functioning as if nothing happened. But I have seen people completely lose it for months over the death of a close friend, and others who seemed relatively unscathed by the death of their own mother. It got me wondering, what accounts for this disparity? Why *do* we feel some losses more deeply? How can one death seem survivable, but multiple deaths in a short period of time throw us into a tailspin?

I believe that part of the answer to those questions lies not in the defined relationship you had with the departed, but in the impact the loss has on you and on your life.

Did the loss touch the life of someone who is close to you, and you are grieving on their behalf? This can be very difficult and is one of the least recognized forms of grief.

Did the loss touch you in a way that affects your outlook on life? Examples of this might be the school shootings or the September 11 terrorist attacks, events which shake our sense of security or cause us a crisis of faith with our God.

Did the loss change your day to day routine, by taking away someone whom you dealt with in an intimate way, such as a parent or sibling? The more our daily routine was influenced by or involved the one who died, the more reminders we have and the longer it takes to adapt to their absence from our lives (This is one reason that the loss of a pet can be such a profoundly painful experience).

Perhaps most difficult, did the loss change *you*? Many people who have lost a child or a spouse express the sense that a part of them died along with their loved one. That is certainly how it feels.

I wish I could offer more answers than questions! Believe me; I would share them with you. What I do know is this:

No matter how a death affects us, we must be more patient with ourselves

It is time as a society for us to stop repressing grief and making people feel weak and inadequate when they don't bounce back in some pre-determined amount of time. The fact is, this is one of the most universal experiences in human existence and we have to give ourselves permission to grieve freely. Our reactions, whatever they are, are part of a normal, healthy response to facing our own mortality and our own lack of control over the world we live in. Death is the ultimate wake-up call. The closer to home it hits us, the longer it takes to recover.

In my grief process, I experienced all of the following reactions and feelings...thank God not all at the same time.

INSOMNIA

I am not exaggerating—my eyes stayed open for ten days after Jack died, through the week of his funeral, and immediately after my mother found out that she also had malignant cancer. I was totally exhausted. I was crying at the drop of a hat. But I could *not* sleep. I would lie down, wishing for the blessed relief of being oblivious for even a few minutes, but I remained wide awake. My brain was on complete and total overload. I think I was trying to rely on old instincts, as if what was happening was a problem to be solved, even though I knew in my heart and soul that there was no solution. But still, I worked the problem. And stayed awake. In desperation, I called my doctor and told him what was happening. He prescribed a sleep aid and the first night I took it I slept for ten hours. Every night after that for the ten days of pills he gave me, I slept hard as a rock. I called and begged him for a thirty day supply, knowing that in order to give my mother the help she needed with her chemo and radiation, I had to have sleep. Needless to say, I became addicted to the sleeping pills and had to seek help to ease off them in the months to come.

TEARS

In the first several days after each of my losses, I got caught off guard by a sudden welling of tears that were triggered by absolutely *any* reminder of my loved ones. Every night at 10:00 p.m. for three months after Jack died, I closed my bedroom door, sat down on the floor, and stared at his picture, listening to music about losing a spouse. For months, I marked the time he died each Thursday night at exactly seven minutes after midnight. Over time, this ritual became important only on the monthly anniversary of the night he died. Regardless of how often I grieved in this way, I relived the moments leading up to his last breath in a private tribute which always ended with me crying so hard I often feared I would not be able to stop. I had no idea this was even possible, but I actually burst an eardrum one night from sobbing so hard. This was how I dealt with the physical pain in my chest that gradually built each day until it developed a will of its own and would no longer be denied. Now, over three years later, I am still occasionally caught off-guard by a sudden memory and I burst into tears.

TERROR

Knowing Jack was going to die after we had spent every ounce of energy trying to prevent it left me completely terrified. The feeling of being left behind, of having to face life without anchors—was very frightening. I remember hyperventilating and having heart palpitations when the fear of being alone hit me. I felt powerless to stop it.

LOSS OF APPETITE

Forgetting to eat a meal every once in a while seems pretty harmless. Losing some weight after a loss is very common. (Or gaining weight, it all depends on how your body reacts to stress). But in my case, my loss of appetite and resulting weight loss was because food no longer had any taste. I derived no enjoyment from eating, and I started to become thin to the extent that my grief counselor got very concerned. She actually assigned me "homework" one week to "eat three meals a day, whether you are hungry or not." I realized that the day I stopped eating tied back to when Jack stopped eating at the end, in preparation for dying. I was so connected to him emotionally, I stopped needing or wanting food; unfortunately, this lasted well beyond his death.

AWE

Not all of my reactions were horrifying or depressing. At one point, listening to Jack chuckle at his own joke when he was in his last stages of life, I was overcome with awe by the power of the human spirit to hold on after the body has wasted away to almost nothing. I learned that this is one of the gifts that being in hospice can give us, if we have the strength to stay by the side of one who is dying.

ALL IS ONE

I felt at one with the universe as I realized how death is as natural as birth, and all part of a mysterious cycle played out by every living creature.

"I SEEK DEAD PEOPLE"

Forgive the modest attempt at humor here, but seriously, I'm sure my efforts to connect to my lost loved ones were amusing, if not outright laughable. After Dad died, I felt compelled to be near him, especially since I didn't get to say goodbye. So, I started frequenting cemeteries. I guess it sounds pretty weird, but I would often get my lunch from a drive-through fast food place and drive out to a local cemetery to eat (any one would do, since I couldn't get to where his ashes were buried, four states away). I took my son with me one time and he was totally freaked out. He just couldn't understand how I got comfort by doing that. Later, after Jack died, I gathered nearly everything he had ever given me and placed them one by one in a certain spot on the floor of my bedroom, next to his picture from the memorial service. Every time I needed to feel close to him, I would go to that place, and sit and cry, or sit and think, or sit and do nothing at all. I played music we had last listened to, I splashed his cologne on my wrists and closed my eyes and imagined him there next to me. I wore his clothes. When those things didn't give me the hoped for comfort, I would drive over to the old house and try to get in. I no longer had a key to the home we shared and the new owners hadn't moved in yet. I was desperate to get inside to the place where we spent those last weeks together. I actually went there after dark one night with a flashlight and broke-in through a back door, just to sit in the empty bedroom where I had been with him when he died. I visited cities we had vacationed in; I read books written by authors we had both enjoyed; I tried nearly everything trying to recapture the feeling I had when we were together. Needless to say, none of it actually worked, but it was over a year before I stopped trying.

VULNERABILITY

I went from feeling completely invincible, to thinking I could die at any moment. Every headache was a brain tumor, as yet undiagnosed. I stopped wondering *if* I would get cancer and started wondering which kind it was going to be. This led to an unanticipated response, that of an attack of...

OBSESSION WITH MY OWN DEATH

After experiencing firsthand the "paperwork of death" as my father's executor, I became maniacally fixated on getting my own affairs in order. I literally spent every day for weeks getting some part of my life more orderly in case of my own sudden demise. I updated my will, I got beneficiaries in place on all my accounts, I went through filing cabinets and closets and threw away anything that I didn't want my own children to have to sort through and deal with. It was obsessive, and I knew it. But it seemed to me to be extremely important and urgent. Who knew? I could be killed today in a car accident. How would my family ever find anything in the mess I called my office at home? In a flash of insight, I suddenly understood *exactly* why so many older people have their grave sites picked out and their funeral expenses pre-paid. They weren't being morbid, they were being thoughtful!

IMPATIENCE with anyone who TOOK LIFE FOR GRANTED

This reaction was most evident during a conversation I remember having with my son and daughter not long after *everyone died*, as we had come to describe those eighteen months. We were standing in the kitchen, and the kids were bickering at each other and it was getting increasingly personal and harsh. They started saying those things that siblings often say to each other, like "I'll be so glad when you go away to college, I won't have to listen to you anymore," and "Are you kidding, I can't *wait* to get away from you and get on my own." I lost it. I came completely unglued. At the top of my lungs, I yelled at them to "Stop it!" "Don't you realize?" I shrieked at my son. "Your sister could get killed in a car accident on her way to college and that will have been the last thing you ever said to her!" To my daughter, I said, "Melody, for heaven sakes, what if you never see your brother again, is that how you want to remember your last moments together?" They looked at me like the lunatic I had become, and my daughter said quietly, with a trace of amusement, "Mom, we're not going to die." "What do you mean 'you're not going to die'?" I screamed. "**We're all going to die!**" Later on, in a more sane time, this became known affectionately as "Mom's 'We're All Going to Die' Speech." But the message was clear. How *dare* you take life and loved ones for granted, after all we've been through?

DEPRESSION

I no longer use this word lightly, because it means a great deal more than sad, although of course I felt sadness many,

many times, in the past months and years. The depression I'm talking about here is a serious, physical reaction to emotional turmoil; it can be completely debilitating. I have a friend who remembered that she went for weeks without bathing after her mother died, not because she didn't want to, but because it never even occurred to her that she hadn't. In my own case, I kept up a good front, but my grief counselor saw through the mask, and realized that I was slipping into a very dark place. Depression is perhaps most aptly described as the complete absence of feeling. It's not that you are sad all the time. On the contrary, depression is the inability to feel anything, joy, sadness, relief, anger, anything. When my daughter graduated high school, I genuinely expected to feel lots of things— joy and celebration, mixed with feelings of pride in her accomplishments, perhaps the bitter longing for the loved ones who weren't there to share the moment. But I went through the evening graduation ceremony feeling utterly detached, like I was observing strangers. I was aware of how odd it was, but for the life of me I couldn't feel a thing. Eventually, I came to realize that this unhealthy state needed to be addressed and I sought treatment from a psychiatrist.

POST TRAUMATIC STRESS DISORDER

This may be less common, but I was glad to have someone (in this case, a psychiatrist) give a name to a collection of feelings and physical symptoms, which reached a peak a couple of months after Mom died. As a well paid professional in a job that required a high level of creativity and energy, I quickly found that I was unable to do an adequate job as the company's corporate advocate for women in technology programs. On the verge of collapse, I sought a three month medical leave, and it was granted. The story of my PTSD is too long to retell, but for now let me just say that while I still jump at the sound of a sudden movement or a noise (exaggerated startle reflex), the other symptoms are all gone. I no longer wake up in a cold sweat in the middle of the night, with an unspecified feeling of dread. Medical dramas on TV do not induce sudden flashbacks of what it was like to watch both my parents and the love of my life take their last breaths. I do not have difficulty concentrating or have trouble breathing or avoid hospital waiting rooms. I do, however, still take my Zoloft and may do that for a very long time to come.

OBSESSION WITH WHO WOULD DIE NEXT

One of things that no one really prepares you for is how death can cause you to question everything you thought you understood about life. The randomness of it all, the seeming lack of any order or fairness, can bring about a sense of purposelessness that is hard to describe. My response to this sea of uncertainty was to take a rather abnormally pragmatic approach. I came to see death as the MOST predictable thing that can happen in our lives. Somebody I know *is* going to be the next to go. This is an indisputable fact. I started to spend time thinking about it in terms of "Who's Next?" Could it be one of my children? I was sure I wouldn't survive that, so I tried very hard not to dwell on that possibility. Or would it be Jack's ninety-year-old mother, who had surprised everyone with her longevity and ability to overcome a variety of health crises? Perhaps it would come from a completely random place, like an airplane crash on one of my brother's many overseas trips, or an attack of anthrax at my sister's newspaper. Or perhaps a more mundane, typical sort of end to someone's life, like a heart attack felling my boss, or one of my good friends. This became so intellectually intriguing to me that I couldn't help noticing when *no one* died in my sphere of close acquaintances for an entire year. My son thought I had really gone over the edge when I raised my glass to toast on New Year's Eve one year with the words, "Well, here's to 2003, the year nobody close to us died." I thought that was really something!

So, I hope that you will keep this list of responses in mind, along with the other stories I will relay to you in the coming chapters, and be patient with yourself if you are grieving. It takes a very, very long time to heal the wounds of the soul, and you must give yourself permission to go through this process without recriminations, regret, or guilt.

Go forth, and grieve to your heart's content

CHAPTER 2
The Need for Responsibility-Free Time

O K, so you've given yourself permission to grieve freely, even established a conviction that it is your right as a human being. In order to process grief effectively, we can help ourselves by carving out something I like to call "Responsibility-Free" time. This is something very few of us normally do for ourselves without feeling guilty, but it is what every grieving person craves. The brain is on such complete overload with the new questions and doubts and fears about life after the loss, and our deepest yearning is often to simply have time to sit and *think*. The intense need to be left alone is a healthy and normal reaction. But there seems to be no end to the busywork and tasks that can occupy us, so we don't have to consider these questions, not to mention well-meaning people who are afraid to leave us alone. In order to give ourselves the gift of "responsibility-free time," we may need to plan time off from work, perhaps even find a way to get away from our usual home environment.

Why is Responsibility-Free time so important?

This is important because of the unending series of projects, chores and tasks, not to mention family members, phones, computers, and TV's that try to pull us away and interrupt our thoughts. We must be responsible for nothing but our own comfort during these special times, so that the natural process of grieving can occur.

Remember, the purpose is not to get your mind OFF of your sadness and confusion. The purpose is to have nothing to distract you from it at all.

I know a woman recovering from the loss of both of her parents who had the means to treat herself to a resort/spa destination when she needed to be alone. I highly recommend this option because of the focus on health, exercise, and pampering that permeates every spa experience. If you can possibly do this for yourself, even for just a day or two, make it happen.

But we don't need to spend money to flee our responsibilities and have time to ourselves. Camping out, going for long drives, spending the day at a beach, or zoo, I'm sure you can think of lots of ways to provide the physical and emotional distance that you need. However, keep in mind some suggestions for what you do NOT need as you seek this time alone.

Suggested Don'ts when you need to get away from it all

Don't fall into the trap of visiting friends or relatives. No matter how wonderful they are, their problems, day-to-day schedules, and mere presence will interfere with your ability to focus solely on YOU. Plus, the energy expended trying to assure everyone that you are "OK" will wear you out.

Don't make excuses for why you can wait to do this. I've met any number of people who agree that this is a good idea, but have a million and one reasons why it can wait until it's convenient. Trust me; this is avoidance pure and simple. Stop thinking of the best time to get away and see if you can figure out the absolute *soonest* you can get away. Treat this as a necessary step in your healing process, not as a luxury.

Don't assume a few long drives in the country or a couple of extra rounds of golf are going to suffice. Underestimating our own need for solitude is a very common mistake. I remember when I was at my most distraught, my grief counselor insisted I find a way to get time to myself and she didn't rest until I brought her a plan to go away for an entire week. This was while my mother was ill and I had to hire people to care for her 24 hours a day while I was gone. Little did I know that I would later need more and more time for myself.

Don't feel bad about asking people to cover for you while you are gone. This one is really tough, I know. Remember all those well-intentioned friends and relatives at the funeral who echoed that refrain, "Please let me know if there is anything I can do to help?" Well, it may have been said at a time when you didn't know how to respond, but you need help now. *Let them help you* by bringing in your mail and newspapers. Let them feed your fish and walk your dog. I'll bet someone will even watch your children for you if you explain that you need some time to get away and sort things out after your loss.

Don't get fooled by the excuse that you can't leave right now—that "my kids need me" or "there's so much going on at work right now." Consider how they will manage if you *don't* take care of yourself and you end up missing weeks or months of work due to a serious illness brought on by stress. Or worse, the long term impact on your family because you have a mental breakdown. Impossible, you say? Maybe so. But why take the chance?

Don't go empty-handed. It's one thing to intentionally insulate yourself from your day-to-day obligations and responsibilities so you can focus on resting, thinking, and healing. But bring some tools along with you when you go. Some people like to bring a journal and record their deepest thoughts and feelings in a safe place that only they need see. Others bring a book that touches on the subject of grief and loss, either as a catalyst for their own thoughts or a way to connect with their pain. Music is a wonderful and often powerfully evocative tool. A friend of mine took along her late husband's favorite CDs and listened to them while she watched the sunset. Guaranteed to bring on a bout of serious tears, but she found this the only way to bring the pain to the surface. (If you are still wondering why feeling the pain over and over again is so important, read analogy # 7—The endless wall of pain).

When someone close dies, we feel a part of us die, too. But if we are very quiet, so that we can hear what our heart is telling us, we realize that the human spirit can provide surprising energy for surviving loss. All that is required is time and reflection, and being good to ourselves.

Find ways to give yourself some responsibility-free time, and you will begin your journey back to the living.

CHAPTER 3
The Grief Analogies

Grief has a way of approaching us in many disguises and hitting us in ways we do not expect. We often feel powerless to convey to others what we are feeling, because we do not understand it ourselves.

What is grief, anyway?

We all know that grief is very frightening, depressing, confusing, and exhausting. The list of physical symptoms is daunting:

- Periods of extreme fatigue
- Loss of motivation
- Loss of desire for things that were once enjoyable
- Changes in sleeping pattern (insomnia and/or excessive sleep)
- Changes in eating patterns
- Stomach aches, gastrointestinal distress
- Headaches
- Muscle tenseness, spasms
- Depression
- Feeling of something stuck in the throat
- Emptiness in the stomach
- Shortness of breathing
- Dizziness
- Lowered immunity to illness

(From the University of Illinois at Urbana Champaign Counseling Center)

But, until we experience it first-hand, we may not realize that grief can be so much more.

Consider these less common descriptions of the grief process:

Thought-provoking, mind-expanding
A step forward in our search for meaning
A necessary process for healing
As natural as breathing, and just as unavoidable

While considering all of the things grief can be, it's important to remember what grief is not:

Grief is not:
A sign of weakness
Something to hide from others
Something to be ashamed of
Something that can be rushed
Over when the tears stop

Perhaps you've heard people suggest (and maybe thought this yourself) that grief can be avoided or somehow set-aside by simply deciding to make it so. Mind over matter. Pull yourself up by your bootstraps. Pack away those pictures and reminders, they will only make you sad.

Oh, that it were that easy! But most people who have truly "been there" will tell you that they knew in their hearts that *nothing* could stop the memories, the tears, the sadness, or the feelings of being lost and alone.

People who keep pictures of loved ones visible are not doing it to keep their pain alive; they are doing it because it brings them comfort.

It is in that general vein that I came up with the idea for this book. Frankly, it is not intended for people who have successfully completed their personal grief journey and have moved on in life. Those lucky people might feel it counterproductive to re-enter this world and brave the depths of the stories presented here. No, this book is written for those of you who are still lost in the sea of your own bewildering feelings of mourning, wishing that someone understood how you feel, unsure where to turn, or how to face a world without your loved one.

In this stage of the process, reading about grief will not make it worse. It can bring the much-needed comfort that you so desperately seek.

The "Grief Analogies" is a concept which came to me as I struggled with the inability to express my own feelings. These metaphors are intended to present a unique and creative approach to describing grief, hopefully, in ways which will help you put words to the confusing and often seemingly unrelated feelings that arise in the days, weeks, months, and years after a loss.

Don't presume that you will experience all of the feelings expressed here or that you should journey through each of the types of grief in any particular sequence. Rather, look for the analogy which most relates to your own personal experience and see if it helps you to know that what you are going through can in fact be relayed in words other than "It's just so hard" or "I don't understand what's wrong with me" or "I can't seem to get my act together" or "I just don't know what to think anymore." I hope you find comfort in the simple fact of knowing that maybe, just maybe, someone does in fact understand how you feel.

CHAPTER 4
Analogy #1

Falling Through a Hole in the Ice

Sudden death of a loved one can feel an awful lot like finding yourself being plunged into freezing cold water. To make matters worse, you thought you were walking on solid terrain, that you were being careful. You knew the risks, but you *felt safe*. Nothing can prepare you for the jolt that accompanies the news of an unexpected loss. You can't breathe. You are trapped. Everything is numb, except for the crushing pain in your lungs. Nothing is the same; suddenly, you are disoriented and panic-stricken. Even if you are lucky enough to be pulled to safety, you are forever changed. You don't just avoid ice-covered ponds; you begin to gaze warily at every seemingly safe and solid surface, fearing that it will prove to be as precarious as that thin ice that fooled you before.

You are certain that you will never be carefree again

In order to translate this analogy to a real experience, you need to hear about Janice. Janice is a nurse who shared her own story with me during one of my many long nights on death watch in the oncology ward of the hospital. Janice told me that when her husband died, she was only twenty-seven-years-old. They had been married just three years, and thought they had the world by the tail. Both of their jobs were going well, they were planning on having a baby soon, and they were scheduled to sign papers the next week to buy the house of their dreams. She was not the least prepared for the phone call that brought the news that her sweetheart had been in a three-car pile-up on the freeway on his way to work one icy morning in December. He was pronounced dead at the scene.

She described to me how at first she felt completely numb, felt nothing at all, as if her emotions were frozen and her heart suddenly encased in ice crystals. Then, over the next few minutes, then hours, she would suddenly be struck by the enormity of what had happened, and she felt absolute panic. She couldn't breathe; she couldn't speak; all she could do was fight a growing drive to flee. Every fiber of her being told her that she would not survive this; she could not imagine a world without her beloved husband. She had to get away, to escape.

I asked her if it was anything like falling through the ice on a frozen pond. The shock of the news was like the numbing cold of the frigid water. The fear that engulfed her when she realized she couldn't breathe was like the panic of suddenly being trapped under the ice. The desperate desire to escape those feelings—was it anything like futilely pounding with your fists from underneath the impenetrable ice?

She looked at me as if I was psychic, and I knew that meant, "yes."

We then talked about what an experience like this does to a person: the lost innocence, the constant feeling of being on-guard, so that one is never taken by surprise again. She confided that it took her well over a year to stop jumping every time the phone rang, simply because she feared it was more bad news. She felt lost and uncertain of her direction in life, having felt that everything she had planned had, in an instant, simply become irrelevant. She reached the point where she wondered "Why plan anything at all?"

I thought this was particularly interesting because my sister had a completely different reaction to a similar loss. She told me that when our father collapsed from heat-stroke and died less than twenty-four hours later, she had those same feelings of the earth dropping out from under her. But soon after the funeral, she began to obsess over the fleeting nature of life and found herself controlling anything and everything she possibly could. As she put it: "if it *can* be controlled, it *will* be controlled." Needless to say, this was not necessarily a positive and healthy reaction, but it certainly is an understandable and common one.

I know in my own experience, I struggled for a long time to regain my sense of security after Dad died. I wanted it to go "back to the way it was before," when I was oblivious, and, therefore, free of the fear that it could happen again. It took a very long time to see this, but trying to get things to go back to the way they used to be, before sudden death was a threat and painful loss a reality...this is not the way to heal.

If we will be patient with ourselves, and spend some time dealing directly with our most fearful thoughts during the grieving process, we may discover something very precious. Something that can make us more resilient the next time something tragic befalls us. We might learn that we are tougher than we ever imagined. Herein lies the challenge: Suffering the unexpected or the unthinkable can make us think we will never be carefree again. Merely surviving tragedy can indeed leave us wounded. But *healing* those wounds is what grieving is all about. It will make us stronger and give us the confidence to feel joyful once more.

CHAPTER 5
Analogy #2

Traveling through a dense forest

The process of recovering from multiple losses reminded me of traveling on foot through a deep, dark forest. The path kept winding in unexpected ways, with confusing forks, frightening shadows, and barely enough light to make out the obstacles in front of me. I couldn't see far enough ahead to know if I was even going the right way to get out of there. Would I ever get out of here, ever feel normal again, ever be happy again? Wait. Was that a clearing just ahead? Following the dim path might lead to the clearing, but it could just as easily lead me further into the darkness, to more uncertainty. It wasn't like I had a map. When those thoughts hit me, I did what any sane person would do—I stopped moving in any direction at all.

It can feel as though you might stay lost in the dense woods forever

I've learned that people tend to relate easily to this visual interpretation of grief. One man told me that he doesn't remember being especially depressed, per se, once he made it through the initial few weeks after his brother died from a rare blood disease. However, he was dimly aware of an unnerving sense that nothing made much sense anymore, and that he was approaching his own life choices with much more uncertainty.

Shortly after his brother died, Joel was presented with an opportunity to take a job across country in a new division. He was completely surprised that he was having difficulty with the decision. He had never shrunk from such challenges before. He forgot that he was still wandering around lost in the grief forest, and that it would naturally color all of his thinking, planning, and choices until he emerged. Further, he was struck by the sudden impression that every decision loomed with the magnitude of life or death consequences. Should he plunge ahead with life, in case it isn't going to last much longer? Or should he proceed with caution, knowing that he dare not make such decisions lightly? Facing an important life choice (the inevitable fork in the road), is hard enough under normal circumstances, but when it is faced in the lonely, dark recesses of thick underbrush and tall trees (grief), the prospect is even more formidable. No wonder he felt paralyzed.

I think it is clear that this is one reason why the experts suggest not making any major life-changing decisions for a full year after the loss of a close family member. This is undoubtedly good advice, when it is feasible to do so. Unfortunately, lots of life-altering situations present themselves on their own timetables, and we are forced to deal with them while still in the throes of mourning. If this is happening to you, I urge you to be gentle with yourself. Remember:

...It is hard to map tomorrow's direction when you can barely see today's path

This forest analogy has another aspect which brings to mind a certain universal truth: The only way to find sunlight again (peace, happiness, joy, a sense of security), is to find your way to the edge of the trees (deal with your grief). I've known people who became so unsure of their path that they simply set up camp in the middle of the forest, and gave up ever seeing daylight again. In other words, they stopped before the grieving process had run its course, and stagnated emotionally. You know people like this:

The widow who is still single and not interested in dating several years after her husband's death

The teenager who withdraws from her friends, quits the soccer team, and keeps putting off filling out her college applications, eighteen months after her mother died of breast cancer

The co-worker who says he is just fine, please stop worrying about me, but who hasn't gone golfing with the guys since his daughter drowned in their backyard pool three years ago

The seemingly successful and happy artist who cannot return to the city where she lost her mother and her best friend three years ago, even though she owns a home there and exhibits her paintings in a local gallery

How easy it is for those of us looking on from the sidelines to insist that these folks should "get on with life." We know instinctively that they are "only hurting themselves" and that they are "missing out on so much." So why don't they move on? Why do they stay rooted to that spot?

It's not because they are naturally self-defeating or mentally weak. It's certainly not because they are happy this way. It's because it can be very exhausting to keep trying to fight your way through the damn forest. These desperate souls have literally and figuratively lost their way, and they will need loads of love and support to muster the energy to get back on the path.

If this analogy describes you, please keep reading. You need the reassurance that comes from hearing from those who gathered their strength and made it through the anguish, back into the sunlight. Believe me, it is worth the fight.

CHAPTER 6
Analogy #3

Surgical Incision

He who conceals grief finds no release for it
- Old Turkish Proverb

The following three stories are heartbreaking, but they all have something very important in common, besides the obvious fact that each of these people has lost a loved one. See if you can tell what the common thread is:

A dear friend of Joan's died unexpectedly in a car accident while on her way to meet Joan for lunch. For the first several weeks, Joan's grief and remorse was with her nearly every second. She couldn't stop thinking about how much she missed her best friend and daily confidante. Nonetheless, she went back to work the day after the memorial service, thinking that she couldn't justify staying away—after all, it wasn't like she had lost her mom or her own sister. At first, she dove into her job and felt some comfort in the routine. She went back to all her previous activities and attended her exercise class three times a week. A few weeks later, she started realizing she was losing her temper at the smallest thing. Maybe it was due to the fact that she wasn't sleeping well. It never occurred to her to ask her doctor about it, telling herself that it was probably just a temporary problem. When she found herself having nightmares about the crash, sometimes waking up in a cold sweat, she shook it off. *Nothing good can be gained by dwelling on the past*, she thought. *I have **got** to get it together.* Occasionally, at work, she found herself staring into space, her mind completely blank, and wondered what in the world was wrong with her. She had a suspicion that it was related to her friend's death, but no one she knew had even mentioned it for weeks now, and she felt somehow guilty for still being affected. One day, she found herself driving on a road she didn't recognize. She had no idea where she was, where she was going, or how she got there. She actually had to pull over and collect herself, breathing slowly, fighting a full-scale panic attack. She remembered that she had been headed to her children's school to pick them up, something she did every single day. She burst into tears and cried uncontrollably for half an hour as the traffic zipped past her. When she was done crying, she felt a bit better, and got back on the road and headed for her children's school, worrying how she would explain being so late. She never said a word to anyone about what happened or how she was feeling.

Everyone thought it was so bitterly ironic when Joan was in a car crash later on that month. "She seemed fine," they said. "It must have been a freak accident." No one realized that Joan had experienced one too many blanking out episodes when she had lost control of the car and veered off into a tree.

***

George was no stranger to loss. His parents

had died when he was a teenager and he had spent most of his adult life trying to forget the loneliness and painful feelings of abandonment that defined his younger years. He was happily married now, with a family of his own, and rarely even thought about his parents. He even took pride in how "well-adjusted" he was, considering what he had overcome. In a beautiful sunset ceremony on a Florida beach at his own daughter's wedding, he felt a surge of longing and regret as he sat watching the ceremony. His mind registered the pangs of loss and nostalgia that he had known he would feel in watching his daughter separate from him and begin her new life. Out of the blue, he flashed on being at his own wedding, three decades ago, and remembered how he had wished his parents had been there to share in that wondrous occasion. His mind leapt through all the events in his life he had faced without them through the years. He was completely taken aback by the flood of emotions that swept over him so suddenly and with such force, and he began sobbing like a baby. Needless to say, everyone thought it was touching that he was so openly emotional about his daughter's big day, and even his wife just smiled and held his hand. No one suspected that George was being completely overcome with latent grief over the loss of his mother and father. For weeks afterward, he found himself obsessing over the meaning of life and death, but he felt angry at the very suggestion that he was acting strangely. He began drinking heavily and avoiding family gatherings. Eventually, he sank into a deep, clinical depression.

***

Tasha's fiancée died after a long and difficult struggle against colon cancer. She had been there through it all: the countless visits to the doctor, the months of radiation and chemotherapy, then the long, slow decline as the cancer spread and the treatment began to focus only on easing the pain and prolonging life. Those last several weeks, she literally did not leave his side, and she learned a great deal that she wished she didn't need to know about caring for the dying. When he finally succumbed, she was saddened beyond belief, but relieved that he was finally free from the pain. Over the four years that he suffered, her life had become a blur. She had neglected her job, she had no social life at all, her own aging parents hadn't seen her in months, and she couldn't remember the last time she did something fun. She knew she needed a break, and took a month off of work to recuperate. She drove to the beach and spent the days reading, sleeping and sunning. At the end of that month, she felt a strong need to put everything behind her and get on with her life. Even her closest friends marveled at how she seemed to be "handling it so well". She propelled herself forward, telling herself that it was over, that she had her whole life ahead of her. Her fiancée would want her to be happy, she told herself. But she wondered why it made her feel so angry when she thought that. Immediately ashamed of feeling anger towards him, she dismissed the thoughts altogether, pushing them down deep in her subconscious. She refused to attend any grief support groups, certain that it would only prolong the pain. A few months later, when she calmly took a wine glass, smashed it on the sink, and cut herself on the leg, no one saw it coming. Even Tasha was bewildered by her self-destructive actions. The first time she quickly cleaned up the blood and tried to hide her scars. Tasha knew that cutting herself was unhealthy, but somehow it also seemed to be the only truly effective way to deal with the turmoil and the anguish she was feeling. A month later, a friend found her sobbing and bleeding on her kitchen floor and took her to the emergency room. She had multiple scars and revealed to the doctor that she had been cutting herself on a regular basis. All she could say to the counselor who came to see her in the hospital was that she "sometimes just couldn't go another minute with all that pain bottled up inside of her." The counselor eventually helped her to realize that while it was true that she was releasing one kind of pain when she cut herself, her actions were also screaming out to everyone around her that she needed help, that she was most decidedly *not* OK. She explained that cutters are secretly hoping that if they have enough "real" wounds on the outside, maybe someone will finally recognize that they are walking around with an even more frightening but invisible wound on the inside, a shattered soul.

***

Unfortunately, the extremes described in the aftermath of the losses endured by Joan, George, and Tasha are not that uncommon. However, even if you or someone very close to you has experienced something similar, you probably don't believe me. This is because of the one of the best kept secrets about grief. *We tend to keep the pain to ourselves, even when it is obviously affecting our health or relationships.* In George's case, he had been sublimating his feelings since high school.

Having said that, however, their silent suffering is not the most crucial element that I want you to recognize. It is that when they saw clear signs that their grief had gotten beyond their own ability to deal with it, they didn't seek help. Joan's frightening experience in the car that day should have been a huge, flashing neon sign telling her that she had unresolved issues and that she should probably talk to someone about it. George's sudden lapse into latent grief on his daughter's wedding day in and of itself wasn't unexpected, but when he started turning to alcohol and began to shut out people he loved, he probably suspected that he needed help to pull himself together. In Tasha's case, she only ended up getting help because her friend happened to come along and knew she needed to get to a hospital. How long might the behavior have gone on without that chance encounter?

Why am I telling you this? And what does it have to do with the title of this chapter—Surgical Incision? Consider the following story, and you will see the connection:

> Jose was a very successful attorney who had a lovely home and a loving family. He went in for a routine annual physical last week, and the doctor called to tell him that some of the tests indicated that his gall bladder was not functioning properly. No doubt this explained his recent bout of intestinal discomfort and pain. He recommended surgery to

remove the gallbladder before things got worse. Jose was a very pragmatic man, and realized he should go ahead and get it taken care of, before it became an emergency situation, so he cleared his calendar, told everyone he would be out of commission for a few days, and reluctantly agreed to come in for the procedure the following day.

The next morning, Jose lay on the operating table, aware of the progress the doctor was making on the surgery, since he only needed local anesthesia. Once he heard the doctor tell the nurses that the gall bladder was out and it was time to suture the site, he pulled out his IV, jumped off the table, and ran from the room.

He had decided that he was done and didn't need to hang around for the stitches and the antibiotics. He was a resourceful guy, he had always bounced back quickly in life, and he was sure he would heal just as fine on his own.

In the weeks and months to follow, Jose was singularly oblivious to the fact that he was going through life with a gaping wound. Whenever it got the best of him, he would take a break for a day or two to get some rest, but he always jumped back up too soon and the incision re-opened. When his wife insisted he needed to go see the doctor, he categorically refused.

Hopefully, by now you know that Jose is fictional and that no one would ever be that bull-headed. Hmmm. Except for maybe Joan, George, and Tasha. And all the other people out there who are walking around with the soul-rending type of grief that results in self-destructive behavior. When I see people like this, I tell them the story of Jose, and then I say to them:

Not letting anyone help you after you experience a loss, especially when your health or well-being is clearly suffering, is just like jumping off the operating table before surgery is over.

It's probably at this point that I should tell you that I have a confession. I presented a textbook case of "Jose syndrome" after my parents and Jack died. I was so sure that I could *handle* this. I mean, after all, sure, I was scared to face the world without the three of them. But, I had just done such a good job of handling the illnesses, deaths, and funerals, I was sure I could now handle a little grief. Intellectually, I knew that three deaths in such a short time were hard on a person, so I went to see a grief counselor. It felt good to have a safe place to talk about my losses. When I took extended time off from work, no one begrudged me that after "what I had been through." I gave myself permission to cry, to write in journals, and to sit idly and do nothing at all if that suited me. But when I thought it should be over, I simply jumped off the table and left the hospital, so to speak. I went back to work, and once everyone had said their obligatory "So sorry for your loss," it was back to business as usual. Except I wasn't back to myself, by any stretch of the imagination. I was completely uninterested in my tasks and assignments on the job. I couldn't bring myself to cook dinner for my family. I stopped going out to eat, I stopped going to the movies, and I stopped listening to music. I lost weight, I cried behind closed doors every single night, and I got illnesses every other week. I threw my back out. I couldn't sleep. Mostly I felt, well, nothing at all. No joy, no fear, no regret, no energy. I was, in a word, depressed.

Now, mind you, a part of me *knew* this was not just normal grieving behavior. Well, who's to say what is and isn't normal? But in any case, I knew that it wasn't getting any better, and probably wouldn't unless I sought out, oh please, don't say it, PROFESSIONAL HELP. Everyone that knew me during this time had been telling me, in one way or another, to get help and that I was not healing emotionally. But I didn't listen to them or to my own instincts.

It finally reached the point where something had to give, and my grief counselor convinced me to ask for yet another extended leave from work. Wisely, although it felt intrusive and manipulative to me at the time, my employer refused to grant my leave unless I got evaluated by a psychiatrist. Desperate to get away from the crushing responsibility of going to work every day, I agreed to go see a doctor.

He diagnosed me after two sessions as severely depressed and suffering from situational post traumatic stress disorder. He began a course of Zoloft and within one short week I started to feel the weight lift and within a few weeks I began in earnest what is affectionately referred to as "my grief work." With the invaluable help of those meds and a brilliant and patient grief counselor, I got back up on the operating table, and allowed the process of healing to resume. It was painful, it took a long time, it was infuriating in some ways, but it had to be done.

Know anyone who is exhibiting signs of repressed grief? Maybe they need to hear about Jose. Remind them that they wouldn't stop a surgery before the incision was sutured. And most of us wouldn't refuse the medicine that the doctor ordered if we thought it would help our body through its natural healing process.

Emotional wounds are no different than physical wounds. When they are serious enough—both require medical attention

CHAPTER 7
Analogy #4

Final Exams

Remember in school when you finished a particularly grueling series of tough finals? No matter how intense the stress that filled the preceding weeks, despite the exhaustion from the all-nighters and the toll on your body from the Herculean effort you had just expended, you felt giddy with relief and absolutely ready to laugh out loud or sing a silly song.

Don't be surprised and, for Heavens' sake, please don't feel guilty if you experience this same relief when you come to the end of a "deathwatch" after a loved one's lengthy terminal illness. Of course, you aren't glad the person is dead, but you *are* glad that the pain and the suffering and the waiting are finally over. And if you worked very hard at making the last weeks as rich and full as possible for yourself, your family, and the one who is dying, you have earned the right to feel an enormous sense of satisfaction. Keeping it together and meeting the challenges of an anticipated death with dignity and love are not trivial accomplishments.

Perhaps you can relate to Ann's story. When her father came down with the flu and a bad cough, she provided support over the telephone, since they lived several hundred miles apart. She had a busy life: two small children, a husband, and a fulfilling career as a computer specialist at a large consulting firm. She was stretched to the limit (so she thought) just keeping her family together and her boss happy at work. Her Dad called one day to tell her the frightening news that his cough was not just bronchitis, and in fact the doctor wanted to "run some tests" to see why the hacking cough was hanging on and why his appetite wasn't what it should be. Worried, but not alarmed, Ann decided to get on a plane and fly to see her Dad and accompany him to his appointment. Her Mom had been dead since she was 3-years-old. She was an only child and felt that it was up to her to be there for her Dad. Her husband willingly agreed to take care of the kids for a few days, and off she went.

Two days later, Ann and her Dad were shell-shocked. After having gone from one appointment to the next, from specialist to specialist, from CT scan to MRI to X-ray to the labs for blood work, they still didn't know why he was so sick and not getting better. She kept up with her job using her cell phone and her laptop, sometimes working well into the night to get caught up. The third day she was gone from home and work, she accompanied her father to get a lung biopsy. No one had the said the "C" word yet. Ann was certain it would be some rare lung ailment that just needed some fancy antibiotics or perhaps bed-rest. So, when the surgeon came to the waiting room and asked to talk with her for a few minutes, she was completely unprepared for the news. Her father had lung cancer. It was important that he get a consultation with an oncologist right away.

Stunned, Ann didn't know what to do. She barely remembers most of the conversation from that fateful day; the next few days were equally a blur.

In that instant, her life priorities suddenly changed in ways that she couldn't possibly have imagined. Cancer is such a complex disease: the mind-numbing terminology and the all-important diagnosis and staging of how far the cancer has progressed. The seemingly endless variations on the treatment plans, the decisions that no one can make for you, but everyone has an opinion about. Without a moment's warning, without any planning or preparation whatsoever, Ann became obsessed with becoming an expert on lung cancer.

She surfed the internet and found there was more information available than anyone could possibly absorb, much less understand without a medical degree. She searched for the best doctors, checked out the reputations of the local hospitals, learned to draw accurate pictures of the human lung so she could discuss the details of the treatment decisions with her Dad and with his doctors. She studied furiously, trying to learn what all the acronyms and terms meant on a standard blood report. She found out everything she could about the experimental treatments available through clinical trials, and struggled with the risks versus possible life-saving rewards.

For a very long time (two arduous years) Ann and her father traveled the cancer journey together, and she felt as if she had two lives. She felt helpless about the life she was neglecting at home, where her husband and children were surviving, but not happy about her long absences. Her work life suffered but she took pride in the fact that she was keeping it together and pretty much had everyone used to the fact that she was conducting business from the road, the air, or her Dad's hospital room.

When they neared the end of that journey, when there were no more tests to run and no more treatments to try, when her Dad had lost sixty pounds and was a ghost of his former self; Ann was tired, very tired. That was when the doctors told them that it was time to check into hospice. The doctor explained quietly that it was time to concentrate on resting and pain-relief, and on making the end as comfortable as possible. Ann wanted to run screaming from that room, she wanted to get as far away as possible from that word: hospice. She equated it with giving up, with giving in, with failure.

Instead, of course, she stayed on track, and worked with the nurses to arrange her father's transport by ambulance to the local hospice center. Over the next five weeks, she stayed by his side nearly all the time and became as adept as the nursing staff at changing the sheets while he was sleeping, at giving her Dad a sponge bath, at feeding him when he was too weak to lift a spoon. She knew that some people endured this kind of debilitating illness for years, not just weeks and months, so she tried to stay strong and emotionally steady for her Dad's sake. They shared some very poignant moments, and he told her how proud he was to have such a loving and selfless daughter.

Ann's reading and her talks with the nurses educated her about what to watch for when death was imminent, and she watched it happen as if from very far away. He hadn't eaten anything for a few days, and had accepted only cold water through a straw. When he spoke, it seemed to be an enormously tiring effort for him, and Ann was heartbroken to watch him fading bit by bit. Her Dad had been unresponsive for a couple of days now, and his breathing was more and more labored, even with the oxygen tube in his nostrils. He was in such pain now, he had multiple pain patches on his back and chest, and the nurses were giving him eyedroppers of morphine liquid nearly every hour.

It happened when she was watching him. She'd noticed that his breathing would stop for long periods of time, and she knew that each breath could be his last. Every time he breathed again, she was startled and wondered how much of this she could take. When he did finally take his last breath, she waited, realizing she was holding her own breath as she watched intently for any sign of life. She felt his chest for a heartbeat, but there was nothing.

Alone in that room, Ann found herself crying and smiling. Her Dad had done it! He'd left this world softly, quietly, and with such utter peace. He was not in pain anymore, and she felt such relief. Her soul soared as she realized that she had done everything she could possibly do, and that it was over now. She looked over at his face, with his eyes rolled back and his eyelids open, and she actually chuckled at her own private joke (Dad, geez, you're lookin' kind of dead there). As this oddly humorous thought occurred to her, she instinctively reached over to close his eyelids, the way she had seen it done in the movies.

She sat for a long time in that room, quietly letting the rollercoaster that had been her life for the past two years ease slowly to a halt. When she got up to tell the nurses that he was gone, she felt a burden lift from her shoulders; for the next few hours, she was too wired to sleep.

It was a bit like knowing she had prepared well for, and aced, a very important final exam...

CHAPTER 8
Analogy #5

The Picture that Fell off the Wall

If your parent dies when you are old enough to remember it, you will experience a sensation unlike any other grief. Something that was *always* there is no more. The loss of something so certain in our lives can cause intense feelings ranging from abandonment, feeling lost and alone, being marooned, or even orphaned. My analogy for describing the loss of a parent for the first time is the image of a picture falling off the wall and shattering into a million pieces. The picture represents how everything fit together in your life, and then when Mom or Dad died, it seemed as if you had to go through the painstaking process of picking up each individual piece, studying it carefully, and putting the picture back together. You knew (or thought you knew) how career, kids, love life, and values and priorities all interlaced to form the picture of your life. It can take a long time to construct this life image after such a loss—with a new image that doesn't include your mother or father.

That sense of security that they would always be there is gone forever

Let's look at some examples of how this kind of grief reaction might play out.

First, consider Jeanette. She was in her thirties

when her mother, Janice, was diagnosed with breast cancer. Jeanette was a very intelligent and optimistic woman, and she fully expected her mother to *beat* the cancer. She was always quoting the latest studies that showed promising new results for breast cancer patients, and even got her mother involved in a support group of breast cancer survivors to help her face the mind-numbing series of treatment choices. Jeanette's mother was lucky; her cancer was found early and she required only a lumpectomy and follow-up chemotherapy. She completed her full treatment regimen in six months and was declared "cancer-free". One lazy Sunday afternoon while cooking dinner for her husband, Janice asked him to run to the store for something she needed for her famous spaghetti sauce. He was gone for only fifteen minutes. When he returned, he found Janice on the bedroom floor, unconscious. The paramedics arrived in record time, but she was declared dead upon arrival at the hospital. Jeanette lived only a few minutes away, and drove right over when her father called to tell her there was something wrong with Janice. To her shock and dismay, she arrived to find that her mother had died suddenly, apparently of a heart-attack. It was nearly impossible to believe, since Janice had not been previously diagnosed with any heart problems. When they were later informed that the chemotherapy treatments that killed the cancer had most likely weakened her mother's heart, Jeanette was presented with the unthinkable: the breast cancer that she thought had been so soundly defeated had stolen her mother away from her. She was gone and there was nothing more to be done except arrange the memorial services.

During the months following this tragic day, Jeanette confided in me that she was having trouble getting back on her feet mentally and emotionally. She felt as if the one thing she had always counted on was now missing, that nothing seemed to fit anymore. She questioned everything now: Was she happy in her marriage? Was she making the right choice to be a full-time working mother to her three children? Was she even in the right career? How should she support her father now that he was alone? What the hell was important and not important anymore?

Naturally, as these questions plagued her, it made her long even more for her mother's wise and familiar counsel. This created a downward spiral that resulted in Jeanette pulling away from everyone she cared about. She withdrew into a shell of protective breeziness, a superficial façade that she presented to her family and her co-workers. Underneath, she was slowly, but surely working the puzzle. She was desperate to have her life back on track and not feel so lost. One by one, she examined her life choices and her current circumstances. She began to find ways to cope with how to get by in her world without daily contact with her touchstone, her mother. She created a photo album for her children with many great snapshots of them with their grandmother, and encouraged them to talk about her and to remember the times they shared. She began to write in a journal when she felt the need to talk to her mother about something, even supplying her mother's typical replies, as best she could. "What would Mom say?" became her new mantra. She took a vacation from work and went with her husband for a quiet oceanside getaway and told him how hard the loss was for her and asked him to be patient with her. She told him that her emotional distance from him lately was due to her questioning every aspect of her life, and she needed him to understand how deeply this was affecting her. To her surprise and relief, he seemed glad to be able to talk about it, and they shared some wonderful memories of Jeanette's mom and ended up comforting each other. At work, she started mentioning her mother again in conversations with her coworkers, and it felt good to have her mother's memory welcomed back into her day to day life.

This process of reorganizing her life around the vital missing piece was painful and lengthy. But it was essential to her healing. Jeanette emerged from her grief-work a stronger person, but more importantly, she told me that she had a much deeper appreciation for the time she spent with her own children. She was also grateful that she had been given as much time as she had with her mother. Her life image, her picture, had been broken. It took years before it was pieced back together and hanging once more in a place of honor on her life's wall.

This story oversimplifies a highly emotional and difficult process, but it does serve to highlight a common and necessary evolution that often takes place. It can be quite unsettling to be faced with the reality that you are for your own children what your parents were for you. Especially if your grandparents are gone before your parents die, the feeling of a history lost can be daunting. For most, the realization blooms slowly: When you were once simply your parents' child, now you must take on the mantel of family historian, or matriarch, or head of the extended family. Many of us take this new found obligation reluctantly, while some never seem to accept it. The cycle of life is inevitable and predictable, as long as it happening to someone else. Don't be hard on yourself if the intensity of your reaction takes you by surprise when you are suddenly without your Mom or Dad. Here is another story about the little things we take for granted sometimes when we have never been without that parental influence in our lives.

Rebecca was a divorced single parent, busily raising three small children and working full time at a local attorney's office as one of the firm's research assistants. She took pride in the fact that she was managing so well since her husband had left them a year ago. Her father lived only a couple of hours' drive away, and he came to see them every other weekend. Her own parents had been divorced since she was young and her mother lived across the country in a retirement home, and was not a frequent flyer.

In the first weeks after her Dad died of a short, but deadly bout with pneumonia, she remembers feeling as if her very skin was on fire, her nerves were so raw. She told me that she couldn't get over how the world just kept on going when hers had just stopped. She wanted to scream at the cashier at the grocery store, "Don't you realize my entire life has just been turned upside-down? How can you be so damn cheerful?" Every day something she had taken for granted needed to be done without her Dad to help her do it. She became painfully aware of the fact that she had never learned to use a drill, hire a plumber, or change her car's oil. She felt completely inadequate to the daily tasks of homeownership, and even though she missed her Dad in so many ways, it was the practical things that seemed to cut the deepest. Her exhaustion in taking on so many new responsibilities took its toll, and she lost her job later on that year. Once again, she stopped herself (for the zillionth time) from picking up the phone to call her father and ask him what she should do. For Rebecca, losing her father was like having the picture fall off the wall, and realize that the frame itself was forever broken as well. Rebuilding her life without the ready assistance of her financial counselor, handyman, loving babysitter, and confidante took Rebecca completely off guard. Until he was gone, she'd had no idea how much she relied on him. She tried reaching out to her brothers and sisters, but they each had their own grief to deal with. Her friends had their own lives and no one seemed as willing to take that midnight phone call she could always make to her Dad when she needed help or advice. Rebecca's world needed to be put back together from the ground up. It took her a very long time to accept that she would have to start doing things for herself. She often was overcome with a feeling of not being *ready,* of wanting so badly to just be the *child* again, and to have someone take care of her without question or recrimination.

Let's stop for a moment and take stock. If you have had a

similar experience as Rebecca or Jeanette, perhaps you are now thinking about how your life has been confusing and "broken" since the loss of your mother or father (or both).

Remember that grieving is a process

You can see how important it is for you to reconstruct each area of your life one aspect at a time, in light of the new landscape into which you have been thrust. Give yourself time and be patient. I've had friends tell me that they went through a loss over and over again when new milestones occurred and their parent was not there to share special moments with them. (Recall George and his plunge into latent grief when his own daughter was married.) Almost without exception, every woman I've ever spoken to about losing their parents admits that it took them years to recover. Many men have presented a stoic front, insisting that nothing really changed for them, that these things are to be expected, and so on. I'm not a counselor, psychiatrist, or mind-reader, but it is my considered opinion that men in our culture take the loss of their mother or father just as hard as any woman. It's just that men are trained from birth to suppress any outward signs of their feelings of loss. Here is one very personal example of this which may provide some insight into this phenomenon:

When my father died, my brother (two years my senior) lived in Australia. He was not able to be at the hospital when my Dad's new wife, my sister, and I were conferring with the doctors about Dad's condition. I remember talking with him on the phone about the possibility of turning off the life support systems, and my big brother, who was never one to be openly emotional, was sobbing on the other end of the line. The crying didn't startle me, since I, too, was devastated by the enormity of the decision. What truly shocked me was that he regained his composure a few minutes later and remarked that he was surprised that he was so upset.

Hello! Why wouldn't he be upset? I was dumbfounded and had no reply. But it was my first clue to the extreme extent to which men in our culture are expected to be ultra-strong and minimally emotional. Since that day, when I encounter a woman who is frustrated or confused by her man's apparent lack of grieving over a loss, I remind her that most men mourn just as deeply and with the same strong feelings and reactions that women do.

Just because men have swept the broken pieces of their fallen picture under the nearest rug doesn't mean that they aren't secretly visiting the room to work the puzzle while we aren't looking. Be especially patient if this could be what is going on with a man you care about.

CHAPTER 9
Analogy #6

Lost at Sea

As I write these words, I am lucky enough to be looking out my window at the incredible scenery along the western coastline of the Big Island of Hawaii. I moved here to live on the Kona coast about a year ago as part of my healing process after my own losses. It often strikes me that the ocean provides such a vivid metaphor for life. When we are far away, such as looking down at it from an airplane, or viewing it from a distant hillside, we see the starkness and beauty, the variety of hues, shades, and the endless expanse. Not unlike life, when viewed at a distance. For instance, when we talk about the continuous cycle of life, the ebb and flow of birth and death, the rebirth of the Earth with each new spring, we are seldom saddened. More than likely, we find the circle of birth, life, and death to be an awesome and beautiful phenomenon. We may feel small in comparison to this immense spectacle, but we do not question that we are an integral part of it nonetheless.

When we get closer to the ocean, we can see its power. It reveals its dangers and its unpredictability. The waves, while calming and peaceful when tame, can be destructive and fearsome when we least expect it. How can anyone have witnessed the accounts of the 2004 Asia tsunami and not be overwhelmed with the ocean's power to devastate?

So, here we are, living our lives, viewing the delicate balance of life and death from a distance, when we are suddenly swept into the vast, open sea. Someone very close to us dies and we are left adrift with our emotions and pounded by the waves of sadness, regret, confusion, and uncertainty. Never mind that we should have seen this coming. We did know that the ocean was always there. We simply weren't prepared for the intensity of it all. Somehow we were insulated from its deadly power in our day to day lives. The movie *The Perfect Storm* illustrates this point better than I ever could. When that small fishing boat is being battered and beaten by the stormy sea, even the captain is terrified by the water's power and his inability to maintain control of his ship.

This is where we begin with the *Lost at Sea* analogy of grieving. It can feel very much like we are lost in a vast emptiness, surrounded by threatening waves and drifting with the tides. We can't see the safety of land and are afraid we never will. We may even feel as if we are in this hopeless mess without a boat, completely at the mercy of the sharks, the cold, and the lack of food and water.

I can remember thinking of this analogy one day, about three months after Dad and Mom and Jack died. I imagined myself treading water in an ocean of despair. I was too tired to try to swim for shore, and as I didn't know which way to go in any case, I simply floated along, occasionally considering whether it would just be easier to give up and drown.

When I told my grief counselor about this, she was understandably alarmed. It was the first time I felt like I had found an adequate way to describe my feelings of fatigue at facing each new day. This sense of being lost at sea painted a clear picture for her, and we began working through these feelings much more effectively once they were expressed.

A dear friend of mine went through a thoroughly horrible three months recently, and her experiences resulted in her feeling much this same way.

Natalie is an amazing woman. She provides home health care visits to hospice patients, sometimes seeing as many as five or six people in one day. She is widely regarded as the most gifted and caring nurse on the hospice team. Her ability to bring joy to the home of each patient and their family is nothing short of a miracle, at least in my estimation. The fact that she also heads a household as a single mother of five makes her almost super-human.

When I met Natalie, she was also consumed with her aging mother, who suffered a number of serious medical ailments, and lived close by. When Natalie wasn't caring for the dying, she was attending one of dozens of school events. When she wasn't buying groceries or paying the bills or cleaning house, she was taking care of her Mom. Maybe you are fortunate enough to know someone like her, someone who shoulders the weight of the world, but always carries herself with a joyful spirit.

She got a call at work one day to come to the hospital. Her mother had collapsed at home and was brought in by ambulance. She was still unconscious when Natalie received word. By the time she arrived, her mother was dead. Natalie was stunned by the suddenness. In her world, death was a daily partner, but it usually came in somewhat predictable ways, with family members and loved ones gathered at the bedside, and with opportunities for poignant goodbyes. To lose her mother this way was unthinkable, and the shock put Natalie into a state of numbness that lasted for several weeks.

I thought this was enough for one person to handle, and so did she, until the truly unbelievable happened. She got another call at work, this time from her sister, telling her that her teenage nephew was shot and killed early that morning. Natalie, and of course the entire family, were shocked beyond words and no one could imagine their feelings of disbelief, anger, confusion, and deep sorrow.

In the weeks that followed, when her ex-mother-in-law suddenly died as well, Natalie confided in me that she felt "just lost"—hopelessly lost, alone, and adrift. Nothing seemed to make sense anymore, and it was all she could do to pull herself out of bed and care for her children and get to work. As the sole breadwinner, she couldn't afford to take off any unpaid time, and she was having a hard time making ends meet in light of all the funeral expenses facing their family.

It didn't seem like much to offer, but when I spoke to her I told her about the way I felt "lost at sea" and empathized about how despondent multiple deaths can make one feel. Her voice brightened ever so slightly when she realized I had some inkling of how she was feeling. Just knowing that you aren't the only person who ever felt this way can be very comforting. I told her that I knew it was very, very hard, but she needed to keep treading water, that this feeling wouldn't last forever. Soon, she would regain the strength she needed to head for the relative safety of dry land.

Life can indeed be very much like the ocean. Both are undeniably, breathtakingly beautiful to contemplate. But they can also surprise us with a darker side, a lethal force. Picture yourself lost in the middle of the vast, unforgiving sea. You are completely alone. No one hears your cries for help; the relentless waves keep crashing against you, and threatening to pull you under. Maybe you should just keep treading water, since moving in any direction could be a wrong one and take you further out to sea. Every once in a while, you consider the notion that giving up isn't the worst thing that could happen. Should you take a chance and swim for shore? You know you can't just stay there indefinitely or you will be overcome. This is the miserable desperation that deep bereavement can evoke. The process of grief is a long and difficult journey. Every day you refuse to be overcome by your loss is a day which honors your loved one's memory.

When you get low in spirit and discouraged, remember this:

> The lowest ebb is the turn of the tide
> - *Henry Wadsworth Longfellow*

CHAPTER 10
Analogy #7

The Endless Wall of Pain

No matter how many ways we try to go around it, get away from it, or jump over it, most emotional pain is like an endless wall. It stretches out as far as the eye can see, extending to the left, right, above, even running below ground. Those of us who are mourning a difficult loss know this because we have tried countless ways to find a shortcut around the pain. The intriguing thing about the endless wall of pain is that life is on the other side. We want to get on with our lives after a loss. We know (instinctively) that we have to get past the wall. Pain is not something we tend to move toward, so we try walking sideways, looking for the easy way around so we can avoid running into it. Of course, walking sideways gets us nowhere. When we tire of our attempts, we might just sit down and get comfortable, usually with our backs to the wall, gazing back at life before the loss. Some of us may get stuck and refuse to move from one spot. We stare at the wall, knowing it is important to get beyond it, but we don't want to actually touch it or even get too close to it. We get frustrated with the way our lives are languishing and try backing up as far away from the wall as possible. This merely serves to put our lives on hold emotionally, and we never quite move past our loss.

Does this sound like you or someone you know? Let's look at some examples of some very well-meaning people who made near-Herculean efforts to get through the grief process without actually dealing with the pain.

Karl was an ordinary guy. He enjoyed life and had a loving wife and family. His job was going well, and he was excited about making his sales numbers next quarter because he could finally get that new set of golf clubs he'd been promising himself. When his wife collapsed and died from a spontaneous brain aneurysm at age thirty-seven, it hit him very hard. After the cards, phone calls, and flowers stopped coming, he realized he had absolutely no idea what to do. The boss wanted him back at work as soon as he felt "up to it" and the kids now needed his undivided attention to cope with the loss of their mother. There was the "paperwork of death" to deal with. For the first few months, Karl remained in a state of numbness, merely reacting to whatever demands were placed on him by his job and kids. Tears welled up every time he saw pictures of his wife, so he took them all down and packed them in a box in the basement. He stopped seeing friends because they always wanted to talk about Sheri. He felt a huge hole in his heart, and he knew it wasn't getting any better with time. When the memories of Sheri popped into his head, as they did with agonizing regularity, he consciously pushed them away, fearing that it would just make him feel worse. He didn't realize it, but he was spending less and less time at home, often hiring babysitters so he could work late. He told himself that he needed to make more money now that he was the sole source of income for his family, but in truth he was avoiding his own children because they needed the one thing from him that he couldn't provide: their mother.

At one point, a good friend stepped in and insisted that Karl go to a local support group for people who had lost spouses. It took weeks of nagging and cajoling, but Karl finally acquiesced. He had no intention of participating, but he wanted to get his friend off his back. When the session began, Karl was stony-faced and spoke in one word responses when addressed by the leader. Fifteen minutes into the session, he was listening intently to the others describe openly their feelings of being lost and alone. When one man admitted how hard it was just to go to that empty bed each night, it was all Karl could stand. He excused himself brusquely and simply left the room. When he got to his car he began to cry and didn't stop for nearly an hour. Really feeling it like that was very scary. It was such an out-of-control sensation. He also realized it was the first truthful deep emotion he had felt in months. He vowed never to go back to that group.

The next Wednesday night, a few minutes before the session was scheduled, Karl was surprised to find himself wondering if maybe he should try it again. It *was* a bit of a relief to be around people who understood how hard it was. He knew he wouldn't have to keep up the "happy-happy-joy-joy" front with that group of folks. But he didn't want to feel that knife in his chest again, so he put it out of his mind.

Three months later, Karl was talking with his youngest, Annie, as he was tucking her in for bed one evening. She looked up at him, and with complete seriousness she said to him "Daddy, why did you forget all about Mommy?" He was so blown away by the implicit assumption. He faltered at first, and couldn't answer. He was deeply pained that Annie thought that he had simply erased her mother from his mind when if fact he had been avoiding the subject because it was more than he could handle. He decided to be honest and told Annie that it wasn't that he forgot, it was just too painful to think about her because he missed her so much. His sweet little five-year-old daughter nodded wisely, and then she delivered the knock-out punch. "Well, since she's not coming back, Daddy, all we *can* do is remember her. I think you should try thinking *more* about Mommy, not less. Your eyes have been empty for a really long time."

Karl knew that Annie was right. Not allowing himself to feel the pain had left him devoid of any feeling. The next day, Karl changed his mind about the support group. He began attending weekly and even shared some of the things they talked about there with Annie and her brother. The sessions went on for nearly a year. Over time, Karl realized that he had been trying to escape from his own life. Getting past the pain of grief required the hard work of attacking the wall with a frontal assault, pounding his way through the rocks no matter how much it hurt. What he found on the other side was well worth the struggle. He was able to remember his wife with a smile in his heart. And Annie said she could see laughter in his eyes again. Sheri would have liked that very much.

***

Tomas suffered a cruel blow on 9/11. His parents had been dead since he was a child, he had never married, and had only one sibling. His brother, Jon, was in the World Trade Center on the morning of the terrorist attacks. He had called his brother on his cell phone just minutes before the building went down. His last words were eerie: "I'll be home as soon as I can." He never made it.

Like so many family members of 9/11 victims, Tomas was completely overwhelmed by the news coverage and the continual playback of the images of the disaster. He braved one jolt after another as the initial days and weeks went on and he searched futilely for Jon in the hospitals and morgues. He met other victim's families, but he was unable to connect emotionally with any of them. They all seemed to have other family members around and were consoling each other. Being around them only served to make his loss more acute. It was months before he received definitive confirmation that Jon's body had been identified. He went through silent heartache that comes with being forced to accept the fact that his brother was never coming home. He agreed to hold a memorial service, but he could not get up to speak to the few friends and co-workers who attended.

In 2002, he watched the anniversary coverage

on TV. He was astonished that anyone who had lost a loved one on 9/11 would choose to travel back to ground zero for any reason. By 2003, Tomas had cancelled his newspapers and magazines, he never watched the news, and he had learned to look the other away whenever he passed by the bookstores with their glaring displays of titles on the attacks. In 2004, Tomas hardly thought about 9/11 or his brother at all. When it did occasionally occur to him, he felt an odd sense of unreality.

Tomas was rooted to the spot in front of that analogous endless wall with his eyes shut tight. He wasn't dwelling on the past, he hardly allowed himself to remember Jon at all. He wasn't trying to circumvent the grief process; he figured he could just ignore it altogether. What he didn't realize was that by not diving into the pain, by not forcing himself to deal with the anguish, he had become a non-person. He may not have been feeling any pain, but he also wasn't feeling any happiness or joy. He knew that he was merely going through the motions, that he wasn't really engaged in life.

In many cases, and Tomas' is one of them, it's easy to understand why the process of grieving could be curtailed. Anyone who has to deal with a senseless and violent end to a loved one's life has an added burden to carry as they mourn. Hundreds of the September 11th family members also had to grapple with that awful lack of not *knowing* that accompanies a loss where there is no body to bury. The highly public nature of the disaster added its own merciless drumbeat to the harsh and agonizing symphony that was blasting in Tomas's mind. It's no wonder he simply shut down.

Far be it for me, or anyone else who has not been through this kind of horrendous experience, to offer trite counsel. If this is describing your situation, my only message to you is this—you are reading this book and that is a very good sign that you are dealing with your pain. Anyone who finds the courage to pick up this book is beginning to chip away at the wall. Good for you.

Toward the pain is the ONLY way to get past it

CHAPTER 11
Analogy #8

The Eye of the Storm

Hurricanes have a unique quality. I'm sure that living through the eye of the storm is an eerie and unsettling experience. After surviving the pounding rain, thrashing winds, and dangers of a vicious storm, you are suddenly able to see blue sky above. It seems safe again; things seem almost normal. You start to assess the damages and you begin to rebuild for the future. There is only one problem. You *know* it's not over. Once you have weathered the initial onslaught of a hurricane's fury, you are even more keenly aware of the remaining storm bands to come. This can be when a grieving person develops a maniacal, obsessive fixation on their own impending death. Are my affairs in order? Have I done everything I should do in case I don't come home from work today? Could it be today? What if it is?

Preparing for your own death can raise some eyebrows with your friends and family. What could be perfectly natural attempts to save them time later can look a lot like pre-suicide "housekeeping". When I was methodically and urgently updating my will and putting beneficiary cards in place, my teenage daughter kept asking me, "Mom, are you *worried* about dying soon?" I had a difficult time explaining to her that I wasn't worrying about it, I was just being thorough. However, in retrospect, I can see that I was getting a bit carried away. I had reached the point where I literally thought in these terms every single time I went out the door. I made my bed so my children wouldn't have to decide whether to make it or leave it like I left it ("after I'm gone"). I paid bills the day they arrived so no one would have to deal with something going overdue while they were in those first weeks of mourning. You would think I was terminally ill the way I was acting. It surely upset my family to see me like this, but I thought it was equally ridiculous to blindly go about life assuming that *nothing* would happen.

I know I took it to the absurd extreme, but when I was through with this "phase", I was the better for it. My will reflected what I really wanted to have happen to my assets. I had a living will and a durable power of attorney in case I was incapacitated by illness or injury. Everyone who needed it had a copy of it. My valuables were tucked away in a safe deposit box, and a list of what was there was included in a three-ring binder titled Estate Planning, along with an extra safe deposit box key. A list of my passwords for accessing all my on-line accounts was compiled and waiting for some unlucky relative to sort through when the time came. Piles of junk from years of moving cross-country were finally gone through and disposed of properly. I pared down possessions, gave away clothes, and cleaned out closets. I sold stocks and cancelled credit cards in order to simplify my financial matters. No, no, death is not going to take *me* by surprise! Come and get me, you slimy bastard, I dare you!

Of course, that was three years ago. Little by little, as I realized that life continued and I hadn't died yet, I began easing back into old habits. Small stacks of bills and other odds and ends occasionally piled up and stayed there for days, even weeks! My will is out of date now that I have moved to Hawaii and I haven't done a thing about it! I've acquired material possessions that I don't really need, simply because they are nice to have.

Getting your own affairs in order is a normal and healthy response to loss

Letting them get back out of order is a normal and healthy sign of your recovery

CHAPTER 12
Analogy #9

When the Sun Disappears

Funeral Blues
Stop all the clocks, cut off the telephone,
Prevent the dog from barking with a juicy bone,
Silence the pianos and with muffled drum
Bring out the coffin, let the mourners come.

Let aeroplanes circle moaning overhead
Scribbling on the sky the message He is Dead.
Put crepe bows round the white necks of the public doves,
Let the traffic policemen wear black cotton gloves.

He was my North, my South, my East and West,
My working week and my Sunday rest,
My noon, my midnight, my talk, my song;
I thought that love would last forever: I was wrong.

The stars are not wanted now; put out every one,
Pack up the moon and dismantle the sun,
Pour away the ocean and sweep up the woods;
For nothing now can ever come to any good.

-W.H. Auden

This poem was written in 1936, but was immortalized in the 1994 movie *Four Weddings and a Funeral*, when a main character reads it as a eulogy for his lost lover. It captures the raw despair of losing one's soul-mate. Until I heard this poem, I genuinely thought that no one understood how I felt when I lost the love of my life.

When Jack was dying, he was in a coma for the last several hours. His breathing became increasingly labored and erratic. His daughters and I were by his side, waiting in silence for the inevitable. I was seated next to him, holding his hand, when he took that last breath. I learned what is meant by tunnel vision, as everything in the world narrowed to one reality: He did not breathe again. At that moment, I saw a vivid image of the entire universe in my mind's eye. I was floating in the blackness of outer space. In the center of all the stars and planets, one star shone brightly. This sun was so bright it lit the universe from one end to the other; then, it simply went out. I gasped softly as my own life force seemed to cease along with Jack's. I didn't have to feel his pulse to know that he was gone. Life as I knew it would never be the same.

When the center of your universe dies, everything changes in an instant

The following excerpts are from the journal of a woman who captured the ups and downs of grieving the loss of her sweetheart after a long and painful illness. I want to share them with you because the story of dealing with the death of a life partner is best told in the first person. Her story is hers alone, but it will resonate with anyone who has faced a similar loss.

<u>12 Weeks</u>

12 weeks ago tonight. His last, soft, shallow breath. It seems like it was last night. The whole experience is still a lot like a dream, hazy yet vivid upon waking.

I feel completely, totally, utterly lost.

I'm terrified I will forget. Mike was always the historian of our times together. He remembered everything and told such great stories. Then I would remember, and we'd play off each other, remembering one detail then another, until it was as if we were there again. I keep trying to capture that without him here to fill in the blanks.

I don't know how to be without Mike. But he loved in me the very fact that I was a distinct person, connected yet separate, needing his love, but strong in my own right. So I'll try my best to find my way.

<u>14 Weeks</u>

When Mike died, it felt as though my future died with him, along with my capacity for joy. I'm beginning to see that there is a direct correlation between love and grief. When you love someone to the depth of your very being, your grief is equal in its intensity. If that is the price I have to pay, it was worth it. What we had was so good; I would never wish it away just so I didn't have to feel this sorrow.

But it sure is rough. Sometimes I cry so hard I'm afraid I won't be able to stop. Once in a while,

I'll think of something happy, or enjoy a song, or find beauty in my surroundings. The feeling lasts for just as long as it takes to realize that it is one more thing I can't share with Mike. Even the good things are sad. Christ, I'm a mess.

4 months

Everything I'm feeling seems so self-centered and ungrateful. I'm so sad and confused. I want to feel good again, but I haven't a clue how to make it happen.

Food doesn't even taste good to me. What's THAT all about? My friend Jasmine came up with a quick answer for that one when we were eating dinner out last week. "It's probably because you and Mike loved to cook and loved to eat out at nice restaurants. It's something you shared and something you can't ever share again. Maybe that's it?"

Hmmph. When did she get so wise?

5 months

I had a heart-to-heart with Jessica (my daughter) tonight. I told her I was probably depressed, and I was really sorry I wasn't really there for her. She hugged me and told me that I didn't have to tell her I was depressed. She said my eyes changed the day Mike got his diagnosis and they are still the same.

Empty?

Sad?

Hopeless?

I'm remembering everything now—too much, actually. I remember how it felt to watch Mike lose his health, and each painful step along that path. Flashes of that are constantly on my mind. I need only be quiet for a few seconds and another heart-wrenching moment comes to mind.

<u>2 days later</u>

I went for a massage today. First time in forever it seemed. At first I thought, OK, this feels nice, I'm proud of doing something healthy for myself. Then I relaxed, and suddenly all I could feel was desperation that I would never feel Mike's touch again.

It was SO disheartening to find out that even a massage couldn't bring relief. It just makes me want to get away from everything and everybody. I listened to a song in the car that I never really **heard** before. The lyrics got to me, they were so true:

Oh, that's the easy part,
When I'm alone.
That's the easy part
When I don't have to smile,
Don't have to try.

It's as if the only time I feel true to myself is when I'm completely alone and I allow myself to feel the pain. At least the pain lets me know I'm still alive.

<u>1 week later</u>

I listened to my CD by Beth Nielsen Chapman again today, the one she wrote after her husband died. I cried harder with each song. I pulled out the journal I kept during Mike's illness and re-read every entry over that last 6 months. The memories of what we went through are so incredibly painful. The despair, the panic, the hopes shattered, the desperation, and finally, the resolution, the helplessness, and the end.

Just when I thought I had turned some kind of corner and might get a bit of myself back- BOOM! It all crashed down around me again.

I'm really feeling guilty about the kids, too. I love them so much, but I haven't felt that "deep in your soul, I'm so awed by my love for them, I could burst" feeling in such a long time. Of course, it's not them, it's me. But how could they understand that?

I've decided this is NOT normal grieving, and I'm going to see that psychiatrist tomorrow that Cindy recommended. We'll see what happens.

6 months

Anti-depressants are not what they are cracked up to be. I've tried 3 different ones now and I'm getting weary of the side-effects. The first one made my mouth so dry I couldn't sleep. Then the next one made me so sleepy I couldn't function. This one seems to be OK, but I'm VERY skeptical.

6-1/2 months

A little perseverance seems to have paid off with the meds. This one must be working the way it's supposed to. I feel this weight has been lifted off of me. I'm not too tired to move now. And I actually cooked dinner for the kids last night. It's not like I don't feel sad or forlorn, but I sure do feel calmer, less desperate about everything.

3 days later

Man that was a really weird dream last night. Mike and I were together. We were laughing, I felt such JOY. I somehow realized it wasn't really happening, that it was a dream, but the FEELING was still real. I woke up so relieved that I could feel that way again I just laid there are smiled.

<u>7 months</u>

Well, the plane ticket and this resort cost me an arm and a leg, but here I am, relaxing in a hammock on a secluded beach in Costa Rica and it's so peaceful. I miss Mike terribly, but I feel closer to him somehow. His heart is still with me, and the ocean reminds me that some things are forever. I went parasailing yesterday and it was thrilling. I felt like I was flying, and I felt true joy at simply being alive in that moment. It seemed like Mike was right there with me, letting me get a glimpse of heaven on earth.

I think that being here shelters me just enough from the responsibilities of life back home. I have to re-learn to live in the present. Thoughts of sickness, death, tragedy are far away. Yet beauty, serenity, solitude and health are all around me.

I found that peace I've been seeking. I found Mike here. I love you darling.

<u>7-1/2months</u>

Well, I'm back at work and it's very strange. I feel like it's all a big production and I'm a bit actor playing my part for a paycheck. To say my heart wasn't in it is the understatement of the year.

8 months

I redecorated my home office this past week with a lighthouse theme. I've never been one to go crazy over collecting things, but lighthouses grabbed my imagination and wouldn't let go. I spent hours finding the right wallpaper border. I got an expensive but oh so perfect rug to match (featuring of course, a lighthouse). Over the past few months I had developed this vague, imprecise notion that the lighthouse symbolized giving Mike a way to find his way back. But as I progressed through this journey, I realized in no uncertain terms that he isn't trying to come back, or even should. Then it hit me: The lighthouses symbolized something that could help **me** find **my** way: The way back to dry land, to high ground, out of the crashing waves, safe from the storm.

8-1/2 months

It's been such a mentally exhausting but eventful week for me. Something inside is waking up, something that has been asleep for a long time now—months and months. I think it's the self-confidence that I have something to offer the world, and the wherewithal to change my life circumstances to accomplish something worthwhile. I think I'm ready to find meaning in my life again.

I'm one part excited and three parts terrified, but like my good friend Sammie said on the phone today "Maybe it's just time to get on for the ride", meaning it's OK not to know the destination and be satisfied that I can handle the journey and enjoy not being completely sure of what lies ahead.

Valentine's Day

Last night was really hard. I sat in my study with Mike's picture and lit candles and listened to music we used to enjoy together. I tried to remember last Valentine's Day, Mike was really sick and he didn't have the strength to go out to dinner. He was such a romantic, always giving me flowers and teddy bears and sweet cards. He said "I love you" in a hundred different ways. I remember how he forced himself to get dressed and drove to a drugstore and came back with some chocolates and a card for me. It broke my heart then and the memory made me start crying again. I got the medical records out for some reason, and took a painful mental journey back through the illness. It all came back to me: the tubes, the excruciating pain, the hospital stays, the drugs, the diarrhea, the sudden brief recovery 6 weeks before he died—when he was able to play golf one more time. I read about his last meal of real food, a steak ordered from a local steakhouse and delivered to the oncology ward at the hospital the day after the doctor told us there was nothing more he could do. I relived the sudden decline, the end of treatment, going home to hospice, and the longest 3-1/2 weeks of my life.

I told my grief counselor about it today and he gave me a challenge. He said it was time to find a way to give up the pain. I needed a ritual, an act, some way to let go. Not of Mike, just the pain. I'm really scared to do this, because I'm afraid I'll let go of the good memories along with it. He said I needed to trust him on this, and believe that there is something good waiting for me once I do this, once I let go.

My sister sent me something very special to mark Valentine's Day. She sent me 12 red roses with a card that read:

Sis,

On heaven and on earth,

You are loved

I cried for a long time and felt very grateful to have her acknowledge that my loss is still the focus of nearly everything that happens to me. Leave it to her to find a way to put a positive twist on it.

<u>10 months</u>

I'm trying to get up the nerve to tell my boss that I need a year off. It's a lot to ask, given everything that is going on at work right now. But I've reached the point where it's either that or quit. The timing seems right to me, and the more I think about how I will spend the time, the more it makes sense to do it sooner rather than later. I have some money saved up and can afford to dip into savings so I'm going to take the step. It's going to be difficult to just hand everything over to a stranger and walk away, but I'm going to do it.

<u>10-1/2 months</u>

I've been working so hard, putting in long hours to get everything wrapped up before I start my leave. I took a break and went to the mall today just to browse. I can't remember how long it's been since I last wandered a mall alone. Maybe a couple of years. I found myself looking at this fancy board game, and really wanting it, only to wonder who would play it with me. Then I looked at clothes and saw some nice things and wondered—where am I going that I need that? And who would I be dressing up for? I left each store more deflated and walking more slowly. My emotions lately are like some kind of cruel rollercoaster. Up one day, on top of the world, then plunging suddenly downward, and then jerked from side to side, threatening to be tossed from the car. This is getting really tiring.

11 months

Leaving my job was the right thing to do. I took a long weekend and I'm spending it here at a bed and breakfast not too far from home. I'm a long way from enjoying life again, but I have had time to contemplate where I've been and where I want to go next. I look back on the past year, and there has been such slow progress. I still sob in despair because I find myself viewing everything in the context of "Mike would have loved this" or "Mike would have said this place was heaven" and so on. Our love was so profound, so incredibly part of who we were. Obviously it doesn't stop feeling that way just because he is no longer physically here. Sigh. I think I need to face my fears. I'm afraid of so much lately:

- I'm terrified of losing someone else close to me. A person can only take so much

- I'm worried what will happen to my kids and my sister if I die
- I'm paralyzed at the thought that I am now the sole keeper of all my memories with Mike
- I'm very confused and saddened by the prospect of never again having that kind of love to share
- Ironically I'm equally afraid of trying to find love again. First because I'm so sure I'll fail, and secondly, because I'm afraid I'll succeed. How messed up is that?
- By the way, I'm irritated that just about everyone that has lost their life partner probably feels this way.
- I'm scared to try something completely new in my career, too. How rewarding can it be without someone to share it with, someone who feeds my soul?
- I'm scared I'll die soon, but I'm also scared I'll live a really long time—alone!
- I'm scared of how I'll react if I get cancer or some other life-threatening illness
- I'm afraid that all that creativity and joy and kindness and giving spirit I once had are gone for good. What if the best parts of me died with Mike?

<u>1 week later</u>

I've entered some kind of mental countdown as the year anniversary of Mike's death approaches. I'm becoming aware of a generalized feeling of emptiness, lack of purpose, and apathy ever since my stay at the

B&B. It's as if I stared life in the face, hated what I saw ahead, and retreated back into my shell. I am NOT ready to face life without Mike. Period.

11-1/2 months

My daughter went to her first prom last week, and I felt so disconnected emotionally. I was smiling and hugging everyone, and taking photos just like all the other moms. But inside I was just going through the motions. It was just like attending that baby shower at Carol's house last month. I felt like I was the only sober person at a party full of drunks or something. I could not share what they were so happy about. I just couldn't feel it.

10 days ago I was really thrown for a loop at my annual gyn exam. My doctor discovered some kind of lump in my pelvis and immediately began a barrage of test for ovarian cancer. Confronted with the nearly inconceivable possibility that it would be true, I felt totally numb. The ultrasounds and the CT scan and the blood work, it made me crazy it was all so familiar. When the word came back "it's nothing", I was strangely let down. I think I secretly wished that I did have cancer, because I know how to do that. I know this is unspeakably cruel and self-centered, but I was not "feeling" enough to imagine how hard that would be for my family. What a mess.

1 year

Dear Mike,

I needed to write you, even though I've come to

believe that you already know everything that has happened.

In many ways, I can't believe I actually survived this past year. I knew enough to be very afraid of what I would be like when you died, but anything I imagined was completely wrong. Not wrong, perhaps, but pale in comparison to the reality.

When you took your last breath, it was like a light switch turned off. Time had stopped the day we got the news from your doctor. But as long as you were still alive, my heart was full and I existed in a world where everything else fell away and our love was at its most magnificent, its most pure, and its most strong. Even as you faded and became disoriented, and later, asleep, I was content to be in the room, if just with your soul.

It has been a very rocky road since that night one year ago. At first I was desperate to save the physical objects, the reminders of us. This turned out to be a whole lot of stuff! But where I saw no comfort anywhere else, somehow I found it with the things I collected in that corner of my study. Every night for 2 months I saw down in front of your picture, and I cried. Oh, how I cried. There were so many times it hurt so badly, I honestly felt like I couldn't bear it, that I would die right then and there of a shattered heart. I couldn't sob hard enough.

The trips I've taken, they saved my life, Mike. When I went to the little Inn we used to enjoy, my back was hurting so badly I could barely move. I cried for 5 solid days. But I re-gained strength to face life.

Every time I faltered, each time I've doubted whether I could go on, I've felt you there, influencing me, supporting me from within. I've wanted desperately to feel joy again as a way of honoring what we shared.

But the panic attacks, the insomnia, the stomach aches, you name it, it seemed like my whole body broke down. Going to a grief counselor felt right from the first visit. It became my lifeline, my road map for the healing. I loathed needing drugs to cope, yet I knew I needed the help. It didn't take long to realize that the corporate madhouse was no place for me and I didn't waste another minute there.

So now what? That phase of the journey when I began to accept that you were gone, when I recognized I was no longer happy in my job, was a very scary time. I was so lost. The overwhelming sense of loss became a burden I couldn't bear, and I became anesthetized to the pain. I was coping better on the outside and became more dysfunctional on the inside.

The trip to Costa Rica, where I found peace for the first time in forever, made me realize that I wasn't going to be satisfied until I got that feeling back.

When I went to the bed & breakfast last month, I came to a conclusion. I knew that I would never be able to regain what you and I had, but I could at least recall it. Last night I allowed myself to do that and I saw clearly that your soul never left me. I say to you, "hi, there, so you've been waiting all this time haven't you? I'm sorry it took me so long to get here."

Do I miss you terribly still? Oh God, yes. Do

I wish for those sweet intimate moments when our bodies were one? Of course. Do I long to hear your voice, to experience the way you made me laugh? To join in those spirited debates on the issue dujour? More than ever.

But now, for reasons not completely clear to me, I can think about how really great we had it, and rejoice. My soul broke free from the pain and my heart is smiling again.

I love you, sweetheart.

CHAPTER 13
Analogy #10

Rainbows and Rain

The spectacular beauty of a rainbow never ceases to amaze me. The fact that a rainbow is impossible without the coexistence of both rain and sunshine is equally fascinating. When we are in the middle of the rainstorm, we can't see the rainbow, even when it is there. Perspective makes all the difference.

The simple analogy of rainbows and rain provides the most powerful lesson in the grief experience. In order for us to truly see the awesome beauty of life, to appreciate the things that make life meaningful and real, perhaps we have to have our share of pain.

The philosophers, theologians, and poets of our world have been intrigued with this particular analogy since time began. When we are experiencing the pain of grief, it can be very comforting to think about this time-honored truth:

The sun shining on us is not enough. Without rain, there would be no rainbows

If you're not convinced, go watch the movie *Pleasantville*. It is a lovely allegory tale for what I am talking about here. In the little town of Pleasantville, all the adults are gainfully employed, all the children are polite, and families sit down to eat meals together. When we are introduced to this idyllic 1950's community, everything is in black and white, like the TV show of the same name. Our main characters, a teenage girl and boy from the 1990's, get transported to the surreal world of Pleasantville and immediately their presence begins causing havoc. They introduce the townspeople to such concepts as self-determination, love, and even anger. As the residents of the town begin to experience these emotions, they change from black and white to full color. The message is simple, but very profound. Living a life of predictability without conflict or problems is boring. It is nothing compared to the zest of really living. Feelings such as joy, childish delight, love, and true happiness are well worth the price of feeling some uncertainty and sorrow.

If you are in the throes of heart-rending grief right now, these assurances may seem empty and meaningless. Please hold on to the hope that one day you will reach a place where you once again are standing with the rain on one side and the sunshine on the other. If you look closely, and be patient, perhaps a beautiful rainbow will be your reward.

EPILOGUE
Healing a Broken Soul

Before we can find joy in life again, we have to heal. If you'll allow me one last comparison, I submit to you that grieving is like healing a broken bone. Being impatient with the recovery of a soul torn apart by grief is like trying to will a compound fracture back to health. Just because you grow tired of the pain and aggravation, and *want* to be healed, doesn't make it so. You could get it in your head that you *should* be healed on a certain timetable, but that doesn't mean you *are* healed. Just like a broken leg, healing a soul takes time, it hurts, and it's frustrating.

Let mourning stop when one's grief is fully expressed
- Confucius

As you journey through your pain, and seek to heal at your own pace, remember the following:

We don't "handle grief", it handles us

Society makes it harder on us by repressing grief

Be patient with yourself

Grieve to your heart's content

HELPFUL RESOURCES

Recommended Reading

Chicken Soup for the Grieving Soul: Stories about Life, Death, and Overcoming the Loss of a Loved One, by Jack Canfield, Mark Hansen, February 2003, published by Health Communications. From the highly successful "Chicken Soup for the Soul" series—this compilation of personal anecdotes touches on many forms of grief and loss. Always compelling, this series has produced a number of best-sellers. It is similar to Rainbows and Rain in that it seeks to strike a personal connection and emotional chord with the reader.

Final Gifts: Understanding the Special Awareness, Needs, and Communications of the Dying, by Maggie Callanan & Patricia Kelley, March 1992, published by Simon & Schuster. This book addresses the unique situation of the expected death, and how to gain the most from this heart-wrenching experience. It is primarily targeted to those who are caregivers of the dying.

Good Grief: A Constructive Approach to the Problem of Loss, by Granger E. Westberg, June 1979, published by Augsburg Fortress Publishers. This small but powerful book continues to attract readers after 25 years, a testament to the fact that the topic is universal and timeless. Only 64 pages long, the author imparts messages which ring true in describing in very simple language the way to live through grief and what to expect. Anyone who has been through loss and come out the other side will agree that grief can be a catalyst for growth and can in fact, be "Good".

Tuesdays with Morrie: an Old Man, a Young Man, and Life's Greatest Lesson, by Mitch Albom, August 1997, published by Doubleday. This phenomenal best-seller surprised the publishing world and the grief counselors alike with its popular success. Although heart-wrenching in its depiction of the progressively debilitating illness and subsequent death of Morrie, the book nonetheless was read by millions across the world. It proves beyond a doubt that people are ready, willing, and able to read about death and dying, as long as the final message is one of life.

Recommended Viewing

Everwood: The Complete First Season, 2002, Warner Home Video. This critically acclaimed TV drama from the WB network is a compelling and satisfying portrayal of a family in grief. A big city neurosurgeon moves his children to a small Colorado town following the death of his wife and starts life anew as a single dad. Understated and extremely well written, this series will touch your heart and help you focus on how important it is to deal with the underlying emotions created by loss.

My Life, 1993, Columbia/Tristar Studios. Starring Michael Keaton and Nicole Kidman, rated PG-13. This movie presents an extraordinary blend of hope, courage and humor in the face of terminal illness. If you have lost someone dear to you to cancer, this movie will make you cry—but it will also nourish your soul.

GRIEF SUPPORT WEBSITES

AARP—American Association of Retired People Grief and Loss program includes online articles, publications, support groups, and discussion boards on coping with the loss of a family member.

www.aarp.org/griefandloss/

ACCESS—Aircraft Casualty Emotional Support Service provides peer grief support and resource information to those who have survived or lost loved ones in air disasters.

www.accesshelp.org

Adult Sibling Grief—This site is dedicated to the formation of a support community for those who have suffered the devastating loss of an adult sibling.

www.adultsiblinggrief.com

AFSP—American Foundation for Suicide prevention is dedicated to advancing knowledge of suicide and the ability to prevent it.

www.afsp.org

Alive Alone—Designed to benefit bereaved parents who have lost an only child, or who have lost all of their children, by providing a self-help network and newsletter to promote communication and healing.

www.alivealone.org

BabySteps—Named after the baby steps that form the long and difficult road to recovery from the loss of a child.

www.babysteps.com

BPUSA—Bereaved Parents of the USA offers support, care, and compassion for bereaved parents, siblings, and grandparents.

www.bereavedparentsusa.org

Center for Loss in Multiple Births—By and for parents who have experienced the death of one or more children during a multiple pregnancy, at birth, and through childhood.

www.climb-support.org

Compassion Connection — Contains articles and readings for all who have suffered a loss.

www.compassionconnection.org

Comfort Zone Camp—No charge, non-profit camp for siblings and children (age 7-17) coping with the loss of a sibling or parent.

www.comfortzonecamp.org

Connect for Kids—an award-winning multimedia project helps adults make their communities better places for families and children providing solutions-oriented coverage of critical issues for children and families.

www.connectforkids.org

Good Grief Resources—connects the bereaved and their caregivers with as many bereavement support resources as possible in one efficient website directory.

www.goodgriefresources.com

GROWW—Grief Recovery Online offers a wide variety of grief and bereavement resources.

www.groww.com

Hospice Foundation of America—Includes information about hospice care and programs including bereavement support for families using hospice.

www.hospicefoundation.org

In Loving Memory—Dedicated to helping parents cope with the death of their children.

www.inlovingmemoryonline.org

MISS—Mothers in Sympathy and Support provides emergency support to families after the death of their baby or young child.

www.misschildren.org

National SIDS Resource Center—provides information services and technical assistance on sudden infant death syndrome (SIDS) and related topics.

www.sidscenter.org

Parents Of Murdered Children—provides support and assistance to all survivors of homicide victims while working to create a world free of murder.

www.pomc.com

ShareGrief—Online grief counseling by skilled professionals

www.sharegrief.com

SHARE Pregnancy and Infant Loss Support—SHARE's mission is to serve those who are touched by the tragic death of a baby through miscarriage, stillbirth, or newborn death.

www.nationalshareoffice.com

SIDS Network—Sudden Infant Death Syndrome Network offers latest information, as well as support for those who have been touched by the tragedy of SIDS/OID (other infant death).

www.sids-network.org

SOS — Survivors of Suicide helps those who have lost a loved one to suicide to resolve their grief and pain in their own personal way.

www.survivorsofsuicide.com

TAPS—Tragedy Assistance Program for Survivors is made up of, and provides services to, all those who have lost a loved one while serving the country in the Armed Forces.

www.taps.org

TCF—The Compassionate Friends seeks to assist families toward the positive resolution of grief following the death of a child of any age and to provide information to help others be supportive.

www.compassionatefriends.org

TLC—National Institute for Trauma and Loss in Children is dedicated to helping traumatized children and families restore a sense of safety and reduce the effects of trauma; information available about trauma, resources, and training for professionals.

www.tlcinstitute.org

Twinless Twins—serves in support of twins (and all multiple birth siblings) who suffer from the loss of companionship of their twin through death, estrangement, or in-utero loss.

www.twinlesstwins.org